Eucharist

Family Guide

Mary Beth Jambor

Jacquie Jambor
Diane Lampitt

RCL Benziger

Cincinnati, Ohio

SACRAMENT PREPARATION DEVELOPMENT TEAM

Developing a sacrament program requires the talents of many gifted people working together as a team. RCL Benziger is proud to acknowledge these dedicated people who contributed to the development of this sacrament preparation program.

Mary Beth Jambor
Writer

Jacquie Jambor
Diane Lampitt
Contributing Writers

Rev. Louis J. Cameli
Theological Advisor

Rev. Robert D. Duggan
Liturgical Advisor

Elaine McCarron, SCN
Catechetical Advisor

Marina A. Herrera
Hispanic Consultant

Ed DeStefano
General Editor

Lisa Brent
Art and Design Director

Pat Bracken
Kristy O. Howard
Designers

Laura Fremder
Electronic Page Makeup

Jenna Nelson
Production Director

Patricia A. Classick
Ronald C. Lamping
Project Editors

Joseph Crisalli
Demere Henson
Web Site Producers

Maryann Nead
President/Publisher

NIHIL OBSTAT
Rev. Msgr. Glenn D. Gardner, J.C.D.
Censor Librorum

IMPRIMATUR
† Most Rev. Charles V. Grahmann
Bishop of Dallas

September 16, 2002

The Nihil Obstat and Imprimatur are official declarations that the material reviewed is free of doctrinal or moral error. No implication is contained therein that those granting the Nihil Obstat and Imprimatur agree with the contents, opinions, or statements expressed.

Acknowledgments
Excerpts from the English translation of *Rite of Baptism for Children* © 1969, International Committee on English in the Liturgy, Inc. (ICEL). All rights reserved.

Excerpts from "Letters to Families from Pope John Paul II," Pope John II, 3rd printing, © 1994, Daughters of St. Paul, Boston MA.

Photo Credits
Page 3, © The Crosiers/Gene Plaisted, OSC;4, © Bill & Peggy Wittman; 5, © Myrleen Ferguson/Photo Edit; 6, © David Young-Wolff/Stone; 12, © Jennie Woodcock/Reflections Photo Library/Corbis; 15, © Digital Vision Ltd.; 16, © Brooklyn Productions/Getty Images; 19, © DigitalStock; 20, © Greg Nikas/Corbis; 23, © PhotoDisc; 24, © David deLossy/Getty Images; 27, © DigitalStock; 28, © Ken Huang/Getty Images; 31, © Digital Vision Ltd.; 32, © Walter Hodges/Corbis; 35, © PhotoDisc; 36, © Pat O'Hara/Getty Images; 39, © Digital Vision Ltd.; 40, © Adam Crowley/Photodisk/PictureQuest.

Send all inquiries to:
RCL Benziger
8805 Governor's Hill Drive • Suite 400
Cincinnati, OH 45249

Toll Free   877-275-4725
Fax   800-688-8356

Visit us at **www.rclbenziger.com**

Printed in the United States of America

20443   ISBN 978-0-7829-1020-9

11th Printing.
September 2014.

Dedication

This program is dedicated to
Richard C. Leach
1927–2001
founder and continuing inspiration of RCL and recipient of the Pro Ecclesia et Pontifice Cross bestowed by Pope John Paul II in recognition of outstanding service to the Church.

Contents

Welcome

Children, as well as adults, are naturally spiritual and are drawn toward God. As they approach the Sacrament of the Eucharist, children are in the early stages of their spiritual journey. All family members are privileged to journey with their children as they prepare for receiving the Sacrament of Eucharist.

RCL Benziger's *Eucharist Family Guide* will guide you in helping your child understand both what we believe as Catholics and how to live out those beliefs. The focus of your child's preparation is not only the celebration of First Eucharist but, more importantly, your child's preparation for a lifetime of being nourished at the table of the Lord. Sacrament preparation is not only about cognitive learning; it is also a period of true spiritual preparation.

Families— Communities of Faith

Long before your children were old enough for school or any formal religion program, they were already beginning to grow in faith. They had already been living and growing in the midst of a community of faith—their family.

What does it say to your children when you tell them that one of the most important occasions of their lives was the day of their Baptism? Even though your children may have no conscious recollection of that day, they have seen photographs and have heard the stories about that celebration. When these family stories are told and retold, your children come to recognize, more and more, the importance of those events. They begin to gather impressions about faith and about religion.

What does it say to your children that your family prays at mealtimes? At bedtime? While you may not think of these daily moments as teaching moments, your children are learning much about faith lived in the care of God present with them—God who loves them and hears their prayers. When a loved one is ill, and your family prays for that person, your children learn that God is with us even in the most sad and frightening moments of life. Sharing in all these moments of faith has already begun to prepare your children for the celebration of their life in Christ at the table of the Lord.

How does faith happen in families first?

From their earliest experiences children also come to know God through the sharing of faith stories of the Church. Gradually, even the youngest children are introduced to the stories of Jesus. This is the beginning of readiness to hear and embrace the Gospel.

Throughout early childhood as your children have gone to church and joined you and the assembly for the celebration of Mass, they have come to know that there is something special about this community, the Church, and the place where they gather. Even as very young children they have come to recognize that special actions and events happen there. Soon they began wanting to participate in Holy Communion.

Faith-filled moments permeate all of your family life. It is true: faith happens in families first. You as parents are blessed with the love and grace to foster your children's spiritual growth. Indeed, as parents you are uniquely able to teach your children and train them "in the practice of faith"— first, because you are yourselves persons of faith; and second, because you are parents.

Why does the Church involve parents in sacrament preparation?

The Church views your role as parents in the religious formation of children as both a privilege and an obligation. When you presented your child to the Church for Baptism, you were distinctly

reminded that you have the responsibility "of training [your child] in the practice of the faith" (*Rite of Baptism of Children* 77). This obligation and privilege extend to sacrament preparation.

Pope John Paul II in his 1994 *Letter to Families*, reasserted the privileged responsibility of parents in the faith formation of their children. He wrote:

> *Parents are the first and most important educators of their own children, and they also possess a fundamental competence in this area: they are educators because they are parents* (LF 16).

It is important to remember that it has been within your family that your children have first come to faith. And, it is within your family setting that your children will continue to live out faith and witness the daily example of Catholic believers.

How does RCL Benziger's *Eucharist* child's book include your family?

Your child's book features a "Together as a Family" section on the Scripture and doctrine/liturgy pages of each chapter. In addition, an entire page is devoted to "Together as a Family" at the conclusion of each chapter. This page includes four parts:

- "Remembering Together," which invites parents and children to share what they have learned as well as share their own stories of faith.

- "Sharing Together," which provides suggestions for family activities.

- "Praying Together," which offers a simple prayer for the family to pray together.

- "Getting Ready Together," which gives practical suggestions on ways the family can prepare for First Eucharist together.

Readiness

As a parent you are probably asking, "Is my child ready to celebrate First Eucharist?" Whether a child preparing for Eucharist is seven, eight, or nine years old, that child is only capable of age-appropriate readiness. A seven-year-old can only understand and experience the Eucharist as a seven-year-old. As children grow in knowledge and faith, their understanding and appreciation of the Eucharist will naturally deepen.

What does the Church ask with regard to my child's readiness?

The *Code of Canon Law* of the Catholic Church states that children are required to have sufficient knowledge and careful preparation so as to understand the mystery of Christ according to their capacity and so that they receive the Body of the Lord with devotion (see canon 913).

This requirement would seem to have two parts:

- First, your child must know that this bread and wine have become the Body and Blood of Jesus Christ—that Jesus is truly present.

- Second, your child must have sufficient preparation to allow for reception of the Eucharist with appropriate devotion and reverence.

How can I tell if my child is ready?

Several reasonable expectations that point to your child's readiness are:

- It is reasonable to expect that your child has been participating in Sunday Mass on a regular basis.

- It is reasonable to expect that your child has been participating in an ongoing religion program and will continue to do so.

- It is reasonable to expect that your child is beginning to know the responses and the prayers of the Mass, in particular the Our Father, the Holy, Holy, Holy, the Memorial Acclamation, and the Great Amen.

- It is reasonable to expect that prayer is a part of the your child's life and is experienced within your family as well as the church community.

- It is reasonable to expect that your child has the capacity for reverence that is necessary for sharing in the Eucharistic banquet.

Whatever standard of readiness your parish requires, be certain that your child is never led to believe that he or she has to earn the privilege of sharing in the Body and Blood of Jesus. The Eucharist can never be earned; it is Jesus' gift to us.

What does my child need to learn?

While children may be limited in their theological understandings, they bring to their sacrament preparation the innocence and purity of a child's spirituality. The children bring a desire to know Jesus and follow him. They bring an eagerness to share in the Eucharist. Your focus for the preparation of your child for sacraments should build on these characteristics of children.

The Church reminds us that we come to know the mysteries of faith through symbols and rituals and by proceeding from the visible to the invisible (see *Catechism of the Catholic Church* 1075). This truth is the foundation of our preparation of children (and adults) for sacraments.

Sacrament preparation is comprised of four elements:

● Ritual experience and expression— particularly those rituals and symbols that evoke the ritual language of the sacraments.

● Prayer—both communal and individual, including prayer within the family and within the parish assembly.

● Sacred Scripture—particularly those passages that enlighten understanding of the sacraments.

● Reflection—particularly on God's love and presence in our lives, the power of the Holy Spirit who enables us to respond to God in love and prayer, and the invitation of Jesus Christ to share in his Body and Blood.

When sacrament preparation includes all four of these elements, the related understandings occur logically and naturally. Remember, preparation is about cognitive learning and also about a time of spiritual preparation.

Confirmation-Eucharist

In the early Church, Christian initiation was celebrated as a single event. The person was immersed into the waters of Baptism, anointed with Sacred Chrism, and shared in the Eucharistic meal. Over time, and for many reasons, the celebration of these sacramental rituals became separated from one another.

The *Catechism of the Catholic Church* (CCC) articulates the inseparable nature of the Sacraments of Christian Initiation.

- Christian initiation is accomplished by three sacraments together: Baptism is the beginning of new life in Christ. Confirmation strengthens that life. The Eucharist nourishes the members of the Body of Christ and transforms them in Christ (see CCC 1275).

BAPTISM

- Eucharist completes Christian initiation. Baptism raises us to the dignity of the royal priesthood of Christ and makes us sharers in the priesthood of Christ. Confirmation configures the baptized more deeply to Christ. Participation in the Eucharist makes us sharers with the whole Christian community in the Lord's own sacrifice. (see CCC 1322).

In the renewal of the sacraments that was promulgated by the Second Vatican Council, the Church was invited to restore the celebrations of the Sacraments of Christian Initiation to this original order. This *restored order* helps us recognize that sharing in the Eucharist completes our initiation into the Body of Christ, the Church.

How will my child prepare for both Confirmation and Eucharist at the same time?

Dioceses and parishes may vary in their celebrations of the Sacraments of Christian Initiation. Whatever way your diocese or parish has established, RCL Benziger's *Eucharist* program will be appropriate for preparing your child.

CONFIRMATION

In this restored order, Confirmation preparation is integrated into the preparation for Eucharist. This means that the close connection between Baptism and Confirmation is emphasized, while recognizing the importance of Eucharist as the culmination of Christian initiation.

As you prepare your child for Confirmation and Eucharist, here are some things to keep in mind:

- Sacraments are always a beginning. As your child matures in faith, he or she will grow in their understanding and experience of the Eucharist.

EUCHARIST

- The Eucharist is the culmination of the three Sacraments of Initiation. Your child is now welcomed as a fully participating member of the Church.

- Completion of the Sacraments of Initiation—Baptism, Confirmation, and Eucharist—in no way signals graduation. Rather it is the beginning of a lifetime of being nourished at the table of the Lord.

Child's Book Features

Participation in the sacramental life of the Church is central to who we are as Catholic followers of Jesus Christ. RCL Benziger's *Eucharist* keepsake child's book prepares children for a lifetime of celebrating the sacramental life of the Church. Each book includes seven core chapters, a "Celebrating the Mass" section, "My Prayer Book," a glossary, Scripture prayer cards, and keepsake certificates.

Each lesson contains:
- Opening ritual
- Scripture
- Catholic doctrine/liturgy
- What Difference Does This Make in My Life? activities
- Together as a Family activities

Opening Ritual

Each chapter of RCL Benziger's *Eucharist* child's book begins with an opening ritual. Each ritual invites the children to pray with primary symbols and ritual actions used by the Church in the celebration of its sacraments. The entire lesson builds upon this common prayer experience. (See page 15 of this guide.)

Prayer invites children and families to place themselves in the presence of God.

Photographs visually connect the ritual to life.

Sharing Together allows children and families to reflect on the ritual action and its connection to their lives and to the sacramental life of the Church.

Scripture

The proclamation and reflection on Scripture is an essential part of the Church's sacramental celebrations. Each chapter of RCL Benziger's *Eucharist* contains a complete Scripture story, which flows from the opening ritual and points to the doctrine of the lesson.

Scripture story illustrates the theme of the chapter. The children read or listen to a complete story, not just a sentence or two.

Faith Focus prepares the children and families to enter the Scripture story.

Reflection reinforces and helps the children to see their life experience in light of the Scripture story.

Together as a Family invites the family to enter into sacrament preparation with their child by providing suggestions for sharing Scripture and faith.

Doctrine/Liturgy

RCL Benziger's *Eucharist* prepares children for participation in the Eucharist by helping them understand what we believe as Catholics. It further relates those beliefs to the celebration of the sacrament.

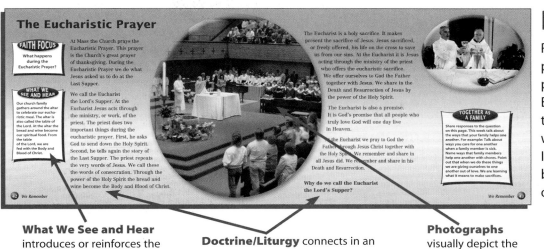

What We See and Hear introduces or reinforces the children's understanding of the faith concepts, prayers, and practices related to the liturgy.

Doctrine/Liturgy connects in an age-appropriate way the teachings of the Church with the liturgical rite to help prepare the children to participate consciously, actively, and fully in the celebration of the sacrament.

Photographs visually depict the sacramental rites.

What Difference Does This Make in My Life?

This page is at the heart of the program because it helps to fine-tune the children's ability to view and make a decision to live all aspects of daily life through eyes of faith.

Opening Paragraph summarizes what the children have learned in the chapter.

Activities reinforce the children's understanding of the faith theme of the chapter and connect it to the children's lives.

My Faith Choice invites the children to make a decision to live what they have learned—to put their faith into practice and experience the difference that living their faith makes for their lives and the lives of others.

Together as a Family

Family involvement is built into every chapter of the child's book. Each chapter has a "Together as a Family" page, in addition to the "Together as a Family" feature that runs throughout the chapter. The "Together as a Family" page has four consistent features that provide families the opportunity to remember, share, pray, and get ready for the celebration of Eucharist.

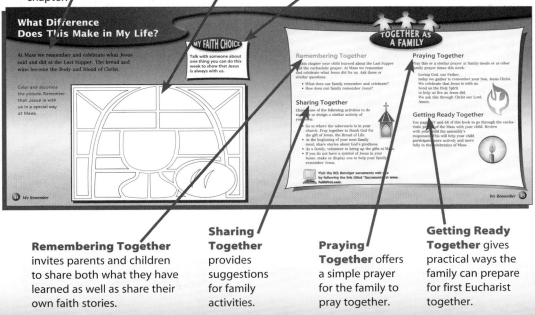

Remembering Together invites parents and children to share both what they have learned as well as share their own faith stories.

Sharing Together provides suggestions for family activities.

Praying Together offers a simple prayer for the family to pray together.

Getting Ready Together gives practical ways the family can prepare for first Eucharist together.

Family Guide Features

Each chapter of the *Eucharist* child's book is processed in four easy-to-read and easy-to-use pages in the *Eucharist Family Guide*.

BACKGROUND ESSAY

A brief, easy-to-read essay that gives background on the faith theme that will be discussed in the chapter.

OVERVIEW

What We Will Learn identifies the major faith theme of the chapter.

What We Will Need lists the items that are needed for this lesson.

What We Will Do outlines clear and simple steps that process each chapter of the child's book.

Looking for More suggests additional resources that will enrich or extend the lesson.

FAMILY RITUAL

is essential to the lesson. The entire lesson builds upon the common prayer experience and shared reflection on the ritual.

SHARING TOGETHER

gathers on one page a detailed explanation of the process for sharing the chapter with your child.

CLOSING PRAYER

provides a short family prayer that can be used to conclude the time your family spends together.

Getting Started

How can we make these sessions enjoyable for our children?

Children always love to learn from the stories of others. Share stories about your own childhood and childhood faith. Don't just tell the stories of virtue—relate the funny and embarrassing tales as well.

Invite guests to come and share their stories of faith or ministry. For example, you might invite grandparents, a neighbor who assists in your parish, or perhaps your children's godparents. Your sessions together should be fun and enjoyable. Don't be afraid to laugh and have a good time. Remember, we refer to the New Testament as the Good News.

Can this program be used in ways other than home-based?

Eucharist Family Guide can be adapted to almost any group. It can be used as a supplemental resource for parish-based sacrament preparation programs. Its flexibility allows catechists to present the student lesson and families to do the family activities and discussion.

When used with family clusters, RCL Benziger's *Eucharist* program allows catechists to group the children by similar ages, while not necessitating that they all be of the same age. The catechists can teach as much or as little of each lesson as time allows, and the parents can complete the lesson at home with their children.

Tips to Get You Started

1. Set a schedule of times when you will meet.
2. Choose a place to meet. Ask your child for input.
3. Choose a place for your family to celebrate the opening rituals and closing prayer.
4. Choose a Bible.
5. Select items with your child that you can use for your prayer environment, for example, a cloth to cover a prayer table and a candle that can be safely passed from one family member to another.
6. Make certain that you always affirm all the appropriate answers your child offers.
7. Young children will need some assistance when reading and working in their textbooks. Offer encouragement during the activities.
8. Do everything possible to eliminate or limit distractions and interruptions.
9. Remember that working with your child to prepare them for the celebration of First Communion is truly a privilege. By learning together as a family, your family will grow in faith together. Your family's spirituality will be greatly enhanced.
10. Make a commitment to one another.

www.rclbsacraments.com
Click on "Eucharist"

RCL Benziger's "Sacraments" Web site enriches and expands RCL Benziger's *Eucharist* and *Reconciliation* programs. Visit RCL Benziger's "Sacraments" Web site at **rclbsacraments.com**.

(See page 40.)

We Belong

Many years ago you chose to present your child to the Church for Baptism. Take a moment and recall your child's Baptism. Why did you choose to present your child for Baptism? Why was this a special day for your family and friends? What difference has it made in your life that you chose to have your child baptized?

Baptism is the first sacrament we receive. Through the waters of Baptism we are reborn to new life in Christ and are made sharers in the divine life. We are joined to Christ, the Risen Savior, share in his Paschal Mystery, and are reconciled with God. We are initiated into the Body of Christ, the Church. We receive the gift of God's love, the Holy Spirit.

At Baptism we make promises that we are to live out the rest of our lives. The Holy Spirit helps us live out the promises that we make. The Holy Spirit is our companion and guide. Confirmation celebrates and confirms the Holy Spirit's presence in our lives.

Overview

What We Will Learn

In your time together your family will deepen its understanding and living of the Church's faith. The faith theme of this lesson is:

Baptism makes us sharers in the life of God. This sacrament joins us to Christ and to the members of the church community.

What We Will Do

Follow these simple steps to help your child prepare for the celebration of the sacrament. The details of this process are found on page 14 of this family guide.

- **Preparation:** Read and reflect on the background essay on page 12. Look over the "Overview" page.

- **Step One:** Celebrate and share your experience of the ritual action of blessing yourselves with water. The ritual is found on page 15 of this family guide.

- **Step Two:** Retell and share your understanding of the Scripture story "The Baptism of Jesus" (see Matthew 3:13–17). An adapted version of the Scripture story is found on page 6 of your child's *Eucharist* book.

- **Step Three:** Discuss and share what happens at Baptism and Confirmation. The Church's teaching on Baptism and Confirmation is found on pages 8–11 of your child's *Eucharist* book.

- **Step Four:** Choose to make a difference in your own lives and in the lives of others by living as followers of Jesus. Suggested activities are found on pages 12 and 13 of your child's *Eucharist* book.

- **Conclusion:** Pray together a prayer of thanksgiving for the gift of new life that you received at Baptism. A suggested prayer is found on page 14 of this family guide.

What We Will Need

These are the items you will need for this lesson. Take the time to gather them in advance of meeting with your child:

- RCL Benziger's *Eucharist* child's book
- A large bowl of water
- Family Bible or a children's version of the Bible
- Scripture card "The Baptism of Jesus"
- Pencils and crayons or markers

Looking for More

These are some additional resources that will help you enrich or extend the lesson:

- RCL Benziger's *Eucharist* music CD, Song 1, "Come to the Feast/Ven al Banquete."

- **Children's Books**
  - *My First Holy Communion* by Melissa Musick Nussbaum (Liturgy Training Publications). An invitation to learn and love the words that we all say and sing at Mass.
  - *A Walk through our Church* by Gertrud Mueller Nelson (Paulist Press). A description of the appearance and significance of various objects encountered in a church.

- **Children's Videos**
  - **Faith First** Grade 2 video, Segment 3, "The Story of St. Clare"; Segment 4, Bible Songs: "Lord, I Want to Be a Christian."
  - **Faith First** Grade 3 video, Segment 2, The Visual Bible™, "The Baptism of Jesus."

- **Faith First** *Eucharist* interactive calendar.

 Visit the RCL Benziger sacraments Web site at rclbsacraments.com.

Sharing Together

STEP ONE
Celebrate the Ritual

- Celebrate the ritual "Blessing with Water."
- Invite everyone to share what it was like to experience the family ritual. Be sure to affirm all responses.
- Open the child's book to pages 4 and 5. Ask your child to describe what they see happening in the photographs.
- Read, discuss, and complete the rest of page 5.

STEP TWO
Share the Scripture Story

- Look at the illustration on pages 6 and 7. Ask your child to describe what they see happening in the illustration.
- Point out the "Faith Focus" question. Ask your child to listen for the answer as they listen to the Scripture story.
- Read, discuss, and complete pages 6 and 7. Pay special attention to "Together as a Family."

STEP THREE
Discover the Faith of the Church

- Look at the photograph about Baptism on pages 8 and 9. Ask your child how water is being used in the photograph.
- Point out and read the "Faith Focus" question. Ask your child to listen for the answer as you read these pages.
- Read, discuss, and complete pages 8 and 9. Pay special attention to "Together as a Family."
- Explain that when we make the Sign of the Cross, we remember that we are baptized. Be sure that your child can pray the Sign of the Cross.
- Look at the photographs about Confirmation on pages 10 and 11. Point out that the bishop is anointing the person's forehead with Chrism. Explain that Chrism is also used at Baptism.
- Point out the "Faith Focus" question. Ask your child to listen for the answer as you read these pages.

- Read, discuss, and complete pages 10 and 11. Pay special attention to "Together as a Family."

STEP FOUR
Make a Difference

- Read, discuss, and complete page 12. Encourage everyone to share a faith choice.
- Read, discuss, and complete page 13. Choose one activity from "Sharing Together" that will help you live your faith as a family.
- Turn to the back of the child's book and punch out the Scripture card "The Baptism of Jesus." Talk about the card and where you can keep it to serve as a reminder of this lesson and your time together.

Closing Prayer

Conclude your time together by using this prayer or one of your own choosing.

ALL: In the name of the Father, and of the Son, and of the Holy Spirit. Amen.

LEADER: The Lord be with you.

ALL: And with your spirit.

LEADER: God, our loving Father, we thank you for the gift of new life that you have given us in Baptism. May the Holy Spirit help us live as followers of Jesus. We ask this through Jesus Christ our Lord.

ALL: Amen.

LEADER: Go in peace, glorifying the Lord by your life.

ALL: Thanks be to God.

Each lesson always begins with a family ritual. These rituals are essential to the lesson. The rituals provide your family with a common prayer experience on which to reflect. The rest of the lesson builds upon your family's reflections.

Blessing with Water

Gathering

Gather your family around a table on which there is a large bowl of water. Invite everyone to become aware of God's presence. After a moment of quiet, begin the celebration of the ritual.

LEADER: Let us begin as we were baptized.

ALL: *Making the Sign of the Cross, pray,*
In the name of the Father,
and of the Son,
and of the Holy Spirit. Amen.

LEADER: God, our loving Father,
you are with us as we come together
   in prayer.
Send the Holy Spirit to open our hearts
   to your Word.
We ask this through Jesus Christ, your Son.

ALL: Amen.

Scripture Reading

Proclaim or invite someone to proclaim the Scripture story "The Baptism of Jesus" (see Matthew 3:13–17) from your family Bible. An adapted version of the Scripture story is found on page 6 of your child's Eucharist *book.*

LEADER: Let us now listen to a story from the Bible.

READER: A reading from the holy Gospel according to Matthew.

ALL: *Reverently make the sign of the cross on their forehead, lips, and over their heart, saying,*
Glory to you, O Lord.

READER: *Proclaim the Scripture. Conclude the reading, saying,*
The Gospel of the Lord.

ALL: Praise to you, Lord Jesus Christ.

Ritual

Point out that after each family member thanks God for the gift of their Baptism, you will bless yourselves with water. Invite your child to thank God quietly, or pray a brief prayer of thanksgiving with your child.

LEADER: Now let us each dip our right hand into the water and bless ourselves, making the sign of the cross.
As each person blesses themselves, say,
(Name), be blessed by this water and remember the gift of your Baptism.

ALL: Amen.

Closing

LEADER: God, our loving Father,
we thank you for the gift of our Baptism.
You welcome us into your Church.
Send us the Holy Spirit
to help us learn to live as children of God.
We ask this through Jesus Christ our Lord.

ALL: Amen.

We Gather

Every week we gather at Mass to worship God. We gather because we, the baptized, are the Church. Baptism does not call us to go to church; Baptism calls us to be Church. The Church is the People of God, the Body of Christ, and the Temple of the Holy Spirit. We are the community of the followers of Jesus.

We, the Church, make Christ visible in the world. We continue Christ's work. Through the community of the Church our faith is nurtured and flourishes. Together we strive for a deepening of faith and conversion to live as children of God.

The Church uses many signs and symbols to express its faith. Among these signs and symbols are the cross and the crucifix. At Mass we sign ourselves with the cross and we see the cross carried in procession and placed where everyone can see it. Through this lesson you can help your child see the cross as a symbol of Jesus' love for God and for us.

Overview

What We Will Learn

In your time together your family will deepen its understanding and living of the Church's faith. The faith theme of this lesson is:

> God calls our church family together to celebrate Mass. At Mass we worship God. We give thanks to God, listen to God's Word, and break bread as the first Christians did.

What We Will Do

Follow these simple steps to help your child prepare for the celebration of the sacrament. The details of this process are found on page 18 of this family guide.

- **Preparation:** Read and reflect on the background essay on page 16. Look over the "Overview" page.

- **Step One:** Celebrate and share your experience of the ritual action of processing behind a cross. The ritual is found on page 19 of this family guide.

- **Step Two:** Retell and share your understanding of the Scripture story "The First Christians" (see Acts of the Apostles 2:41–47). An adapted version of this Scripture story is found on page 16 of your child's *Eucharist* book.

- **Step Three:** Discuss and share how your family can participate more fully in the Introductory Rites of the Mass. The Church's teaching on the Mass as the celebration of our church family is found on pages 18 and 19 of your child's *Eucharist* book.

- **Step Four:** Choose to make a difference in your own lives and the lives of others by living as followers of Jesus. Suggested activities are found on pages 20 and 21 of your child's *Eucharist* book.

- **Conclusion:** Pray together for help to live as children of God. A suggested prayer is found on page 18 of this family guide.

What We Will Need

These are the items you will need for this lesson. Take the time to gather them in advance of meeting with your child:

- RCL Benziger's *Eucharist* child's book
- A crucifix or cross
- Family Bible or a children's version of the Bible
- Scripture card "The First Christians"
- Pencils

Looking for More

These are some additional resources that will help you enrich or extend the lesson:

- RCL Benziger's *Eucharist* music CD, Song 2, "Table of Plenty."

- **Children's Books**
  —*Birthday Blizzard* by Bonnie Pryor (Morrow Junior Books). A huge blizzard cancels a birthday party, but unexpected visitors arrive to create a winter picnic.
  —*Child's Guide to the Mass* by Sue Stanton (Paulist Press). An engaging guide through the parts of the Mass to help children understand and appreciate the Mass.

- **Children's Videos**
  —*Amanda Goes to Mass* (Twenty-third Publications).
  —*Mass for Young Children*, Parts 1 and 2 (Franciscan Media).
  —*My Father's House* (Franciscan Media).

- RCL Benziger's *Eucharist* interactive calendar.

Visit the RCL Benziger sacraments Web site at rclbsacraments.com.

Sharing Together

STEP ONE
Celebrate the Ritual

- Celebrate the ritual "Gathering at the Cross."
- Invite everyone to share what it was like to experience the family ritual. Be sure to affirm all responses.
- Open the child's book to pages 14 and 15. Ask your child to describe what they see happening in the photographs.
- Read, discuss, and complete the rest of page 15.

STEP TWO
Share the Scripture Story

- Look at the illustration on pages 16 and 17. Ask your child to describe what they see happening in the illustration.
- Point out the "Faith Focus" question. Ask your child to listen for the answer as they listen to the Scripture story.
- Read, discuss, and complete pages 16 and 17. Explain that the first Christians did not have churches like the ones we have today. Instead they gathered in homes. Pay special attention to "Together as a Family."

STEP THREE
Discover the Faith of the Church

- Look at the photographs showing the Introductory Rites of the Mass on pages 18 and 19. Ask your child to describe what they see.
- Read the "Faith Focus" question. Ask your child to listen for the answer as you read these pages.
- Read, discuss, and complete pages 18 and 19. Pay special attention to "Together as a Family."
- You might like to use pages 62 and 63 of your child's *Eucharist* book to help your child better understand and become familiar with the rites and prayers of the Introductory Rites of the Mass.

STEP FOUR
Make a Difference

- Read, discuss, and complete page 20. Encourage everyone to share a faith choice.
- Read, discuss, and complete page 21. Then choose one activity from "Sharing Together" that will help you live your faith as a family.
- Turn to the back of the child's book and punch out the Scripture card "The First Christians." Talk about the card and where you can keep it to serve as a reminder of this lesson and your time together.

Closing Prayer

Conclude your time together by using this prayer or one of your own choosing. Begin by signing yourselves, praying,

ALL: In the name of the Father, and of the Son, and of the Holy Spirit. Amen.

LEADER: Let us pray.
God, our Creator,
we praise you for your generous love for us.
We thank you for sending us your Son, Jesus.
Send us the Holy Spirit
to help us live as your children.
We ask this through Jesus Christ our Lord.

ALL: Amen.

LEADER: Go in peace, glorifying the Lord by your life.

ALL: Thanks be to God.

Gathering at the Cross

Ritual Entrance Procession

With a leader holding a cross, invite the entire family to process through the inside or the outside of your home to the place where you will gather for prayer. Invite everybody to settle themselves and to become aware of God's presence. After a moment of quiet, begin the celebration of the ritual.

Gathering

Alternative: *Place a cross on a table you have prepared for the ritual. Invite your family to come forward silently and gather around the cross. Ask them to settle themselves and become aware of God's presence. After a moment of quiet, begin the celebration of the ritual.*

LEADER: Let us begin by praying the Sign of the Cross, which reminds us of our Baptism.

ALL: *Making the Sign of the Cross, pray,*
In the name of the Father,
and of the Son,
and of the Holy Spirit. Amen.

LEADER: God, our loving Father,
we gather around the cross of your Son, Jesus.
Send the Holy Spirit to open our hearts to your Word.
We ask this through Jesus Christ, your Son.

ALL: Amen.

Scripture Reading

Proclaim or invite someone to proclaim the Scripture story "The First Christians" (see Acts of the Apostles 2:41–47) from your family Bible. An adapted version of the Scripture story is found on page 16 of your child's Eucharist book.

LEADER: Let us listen to the Word of God.

READER: A reading from the Acts of the Apostles.

READER: *Proclaim the Scripture. Conclude the reading, saying,*
The word of the Lord.

ALL: Thanks be to God.

Closing

LEADER: God, our loving Father,
today we gather around the cross
of your Son, Jesus Christ.
Send us the Holy Spirit
to help us remember to follow Jesus every day.
We ask this through Jesus Christ our Lord.

ALL: Amen.

Ritual Recessional Procession

Invite everyone to once again follow the cross in procession around the inside or the outside of your home.

We Listen

We need to understand the phrase "the Word of God" to understand the importance of the Bible in our life of faith. As Catholics we believe that the Word of God, Sacred Scripture, is God's communication of himself to all people. We believe that the Holy Spirit inspired all the human writers of Sacred Scripture. These writers, using a variety of genres such as poetry, songs, narratives, and parables, communicate God's Word to us.

Two principles can help us understand the meaning of Sacred Scripture. First, we need to consider the times and culture of each of the writers in order to find out what the writer is trying to convey about God. Second, we need to respect the unity of Sacred Scripture. This means that we must read each passage, chapter, and book of the Bible in relationship to the entire Bible.

Overview

What We Will Learn

In your time together your family will deepen its understanding and living of the Church's faith. The faith theme of this lesson is:

The Bible, or Sacred Scripture, which is proclaimed during the Liturgy of the Word, is God's own Word to us.

What We Will Do

Follow these simple steps to help your child prepare for the celebration of the sacrament. The details of this process are found on page 22 of this family guide.

- **Preparation:** Read and reflect on the background essay on page 20. Look over the "Overview" page.

- **Step One:** Celebrate and share your experience of the ritual action of signing your forehead, lips, and heart as a sign of reverence for the Word of God. The ritual is found on page 23 of this family guide.

- **Step Two:** Retell and share your understanding of the Scripture story "Samuel Listens to God" (see 1 Samuel 3:1–10). An adapted version of the Scripture story is found on page 24 of your child's *Eucharist* book.

- **Step Three:** Discuss and share how you can participate more fully in the Liturgy of the Word at Mass. The Church's teaching on the Liturgy of the Word is found on pages 26 and 27 of your child's *Eucharist* book.

- **Step Four:** Choose to do something that you learned from listening to the Word of God. Suggested activities are found on pages 28 and 29 of your child's *Eucharist* book.

- **Conclusion:** Pray together that the Holy Spirit will give you courage to live as children of God. A suggested prayer is found on page 22 of this family guide.

What We Will Need

These are the items you will need for this lesson. Take the time to gather them in advance of meeting with your child:

- RCL Benziger's *Eucharist* child's book

- Family Bible or children's version of the Bible

- Scripture card "Samuel Listens to God"

- Pencils

Looking for More

These are some additional resources that will help you enrich or extend the lesson:

- RCL Benziger's *Eucharist* music CD, Song 3, "Óyenos, Mi Dios" (Listen to Your People); Song 4, "Alle, Alle, Alleluia"; Song 5, "We Believe"; Song 6, "Creo en Jesús."

- **Children's Books**
  - *Aunt Flossie's Hats (and Crab Cakes Later)* by Elizabeth Fitzgerald Howard (Clarion Books). A joyful encounter of the elder and younger generations as Aunt Flossie tells stories.
  - *The Other Way to Listen* by Byrd Baylor (Simon & Schuster Children's Publishing). Listen to the message within your heart.

- **Children's Videos**
  - **Faith First** Grade 2 video, Segment 6, The Visual Bible™, "Blessing of the Children."
  - "Jesus and His Kingdom," Children's Video Bible (Oxford Vision).
  - *We Listen to God's Word* (Brown-ROA).

- RCL Benziger's *Eucharist* interactive calendar.

Visit the RCL Benziger sacraments Web site at rclbsacraments.com.

Sharing Together

STEP ONE
Celebrate the Ritual

- Celebrate the ritual "Reverence for the Word of God."
- Invite everyone to share what it was like to experience the family ritual. Be sure to affirm all responses.
- Open the child's book to pages 22 and 23. Ask your child to describe what they see happening in the photographs.
- Read, discuss, and complete the rest of page 23.

STEP TWO
Share the Scripture Story

- Look at the illustration on pages 24 and 25. Ask your child to describe what is happening in the illustration.
- Point out the "Faith Focus" question. Ask your child to listen for the answer as they listen to the Scripture story.
- Read, discuss, and complete pages 24 and 25. Pay special attention to "Together as a Family."
- Explain that our response to the first two readings at Mass is "Thanks be to God." Ask your child, "Why do you think we thank God after listening to the Scripture readings at Mass?" (Possible responses would include: God's Word to us is a gift. God speaks to us because he cares for us and loves us.)

STEP THREE
Discover the Faith of the Church

- Look at the photographs on pages 26 and 27. Ask your child to describe what they see.
- Read the "Faith Focus" question. Ask your child to listen for the answer as you read these pages.
- Read, discuss, and complete pages 26 and 27. Pay special attention to "Together as a Family."
- You might like to use pages 64 and 65 of your child's *Eucharist* book to help your child better understand and become familiar with the Liturgy of the Word rites and prayers of the Mass.

STEP FOUR
Make a Difference

- Read, discuss, and complete page 28. Encourage everyone to share a faith choice.
- Read, discuss, and complete page 29. Choose one activity from "Sharing Together" that will help you live your faith as a family.
- Turn to the back of the child's book and punch out the Scripture card "Samuel Listens to God." Talk about the card and where you can keep it to serve as a reminder of this lesson and your time together.

Closing Prayer

Conclude your time together by using this prayer or one of your own choosing. Begin by signing yourselves, praying,

ALL: In the name of the Father, and of the Son, and of the Holy Spirit. Amen.

READER: A reading from the holy Gospel according to Mark.

ALL: Glory to you, O Lord.

READER: *Proclaim Mark 10:13–14.*
Conclude by saying,
The Gospel of the Lord.

ALL: Praise to you, Lord Jesus Christ.

LEADER: God has spoken his Word to us. May he bless us with gifts of the Holy Spirit. May he give us courage to live as his children. May God bless us, the Father, and the Son, and the Holy Spirit.

ALL: Amen.

LEADER: Go in peace, glorifying the Lord by your life.

ALL: Thanks be to God.

Reverence for the Word of God

Gathering

Gather your family for prayer around a Bible. Invite everyone to settle themselves and to become aware of God's presence. After a moment of quiet, begin the celebration of the ritual.

LEADER: Let us begin by remembering our Baptism by praying the Sign of the Cross.

ALL: *Making the Sign of the Cross, pray,*
In the name of the Father,
and of the Son,
and of the Holy Spirit. Amen.

LEADER: God, our loving Father,
you are with us as we gather around
   the Sacred Scriptures.
May we remember your Word in
   our thoughts.

Invite everyone to make the sign of the cross on their forehead.
May we remember your Word when
   we speak.

Invite everyone to make the sign of the cross on their lips.
May we remember your Word in our hearts.

Invite everyone to make the sign of the cross over their heart.
We ask this through Jesus Christ our Lord.

ALL: Amen.

Ritual Signing and Scripture Reading

Proclaim or invite someone to proclaim the Scripture story "Samuel Listens to God" (see 1 Samuel 3:1–10) from your family Bible. An adapted version of the Scripture story is found on page 26 of your child's Eucharist book.

LEADER: The Bible is God's own Word to us. Let us ask the Holy Spirit to help us listen to the Word of God by making the sign of the cross on our forehead, lips, and over our heart.

READER: A reading from the First Book of Samuel.
Proclaim the Scripture. Conclude the reading, saying,
The word of the Lord.

ALL: Thanks be to God.

Closing

LEADER: God, our loving Father,
today we gather to listen to your word.
Send us the Holy Spirit to help us listen
   to and follow your Word.
We ask this through Jesus Christ our Lord.

ALL: Amen.

When our children are very young, we teach them to say, "Thank you." When we go to Mass, we give thanks to God. In fact, the word eucharist means "thanksgiving." The Eucharistic Prayer flows from a grateful heart. We begin the Eucharistic Prayer at Mass with the Preface. The celebrant or priest prays:

> It is truly right and just,
>   our duty and our salvation,
> always and everywhere to give you thanks,
>   Father most holy, . . .   Preface, Eucharistic Prayer II, *Roman Missal*

You can help your child prepare for the celebration of the Eucharist by helping them develop a grateful heart for God's many blessings and gifts. Help your child understand that God gives every person gifts or talents and that all blessings and gifts are from God. When we share our gifts and talents with other people, we give thanks to God.

Overview

What We Will Learn

In your time together your family will deepen its understanding and living of the Church's faith. The faith theme of this lesson is:

We worship God as the source of all goodness and blessings. God always loves and cares for us.

What We Will Do

Follow these simple steps to help your child prepare for the celebration of the sacrament. The details of this process are found on page 26 of this family guide.

- **Preparation:** Read and reflect on the background essay on page 24. Look over the "Overview" page.

- **Step One:** Celebrate and share your experience of the ritual action of sharing bread. The ritual is found on page 27 of this family guide.

- **Step Two:** Retell and share your understanding of the Scripture story "Jesus Feeds the People" (see Luke 9:10–17). An adapted version of the Scripture story is found on page 32 of your child's *Eucharist* book.

- **Step Three:** Discuss and share how your family can participate more fully in the Liturgy of the Eucharist. The Church's teaching on the Liturgy of the Eucharist is found on pages 34 and 35 of your child's *Eucharist* book.

- **Step Four:** Choose to make a difference in your lives and in the lives of other people by doing one thing that shows you give thanks to God. Suggested activities are found on pages 36 and 37 of your child's *Eucharist* book.

- **Conclusion:** Pray together to thank God, the source of all our blessings, for all his gifts to us. A suggested prayer is found on page 26 of this family guide.

What We Will Need

These are the items you will need for this lesson. Take the time to gather them in advance of meeting with your child:

- RCL Benziger's *Eucharist* child's book
- Several types of bread such as wheat, pita, rye, matzos, and soda crackers
- Basket for breads
- Family Bible or children's version of the Bible
- Scripture card "Jesus Feeds the People"
- Pencils and crayons or markers

Looking for More

These are some additional resources that will help you enrich or extend the lesson:

- RCL Benziger's *Eucharist* music CD, Song 7, "Malo! Malo! Thanks Be to God"; Song 8, "Jesus, You Are Bread for Us."
- **Children's Books**
  - *Badger's Bring Something Party* by Hiawyn Oram and Susan Varley (Lothrop, Lee & Shepard Books). Come to the banquet and bring your best self.
  - *The Rainbow Fish* by Marcus Pfister (North-South Books). The most beautiful fish in the ocean learns the value of friendship when he gives away some of his most prized possessions.
- **Children's Videos**
  - **Faith First** Grade 3 video, Segment 3, The Visual Bible™, "Loaves and Fishes."
  - *Grandma's Bread* (Franciscan Media).
- RCL Benziger's *Eucharist* interactive calendar.

 Visit the RCL Benziger sacraments Web site at rclbsacraments.com.

Sharing Together

STEP ONE
Celebrate the Ritual

- Celebrate the ritual "Sharing of Bread."
- Invite everyone to share what it was like to experience the family ritual. Be sure to affirm all responses.
- Open your child's book to pages 30 and 31. Ask your child to describe what they see happening in the photographs.
- Read, discuss, and complete the rest of page 31.

STEP TWO
Share the Scripture Story

- Look at the illustration on pages 32 and 33. Ask your child to describe what they see happening in the illustration.
- Point out the "Faith Focus" question. Ask your child to listen for the answer as they listen to the Scripture story.
- Read, discuss, and complete pages 32 and 33. Pay special attention to "Together as a Family."

STEP THREE
Discover the Faith of the Church

- Look at the photographs on pages 34 and 35. Ask your child to describe what they see happening in the pictures.
- Read the "Faith Focus" question. Ask your child to listen for the answer as you read.
- Read, discuss, and complete pages 34 and 35. Pay special attention to "Together as a Family." Emphasize that all our blessings come from God.
- You might like to use pages 66 and 67 of your child's *Eucharist* book to help your child better understand and become familiar with the rites and prayers of the Preparation of the Altar and Gifts and of the Preface.

STEP FOUR
Make a Difference

- Read, discuss, and complete page 36. Encourage everyone to share a faith choice.
- Read, discuss, and complete page 37. Choose one activity from "Sharing Together" that will help you live your faith as a family.
- Turn to the back of the child's book and punch out the Scripture card "Jesus Feeds the People." Talk about the card and where you can keep it to serve as a reminder of this lesson and your time together.

Closing Prayer

Conclude your time together by using this prayer or one of your own choosing. Begin by signing yourselves, praying,

ALL: In the name of the Father, and of the Son, and of the Holy Spirit. Amen.

LEADER: Let us thank God for the gifts he has given us.

ALL: Thank you, Lord.

LEADER: For food,

ALL: thank you, Lord.

LEADER: For our family,

ALL: thank you, Lord.

LEADER: For our Church,

ALL: thank you, Lord.

LEADER: God is the source of all our blessings. May he bless us with the Gifts of the Holy Spirit. May he fill our hearts with joy. May God bless us, the Father, and the Son, and the Holy Spirit.

ALL: Amen.

Sharing of Bread

Gathering

Gather your family around a table where you have placed a variety of breads in a basket. Invite everyone to settle themselves and to become aware of God's presence. After a moment of quiet, begin the celebration of the ritual.

LEADER: Let us begin as we were baptized.

ALL: *Making the Sign of the Cross, pray,*
In the name of the Father,
and of the Son,
and of the Holy Spirit. Amen.

LEADER: God, our loving Father,
you have called us to come together
in the name of your Son, Jesus Christ.
We give thanks for the love and care
    you have for us.
We make our prayer through Jesus Christ
    our Lord.

ALL: Amen.

Scripture Reading

Proclaim or invite someone to proclaim the Scripture story "Jesus Feeds the People" (see Luke 9:10–17) from your family Bible. An adapted version of the Scripture story is found on page 32 of your child's Eucharist book.

LEADER: Let us make the sign of the cross on our forehead, lips, and over our heart and ask the Holy Spirit to help us listen to the Word of God.

READER: A reading from the holy Gospel according to Luke.

ALL: *Reverently make the sign of the cross on their forehead, lips, and over their heart, saying,*
Glory to you, O Lord.

READER: *Proclaim the Scripture. Conclude the reading, saying,*
The Gospel of the Lord.

ALL: Praise to you, Lord Jesus Christ.

Ritual

Pass the basket of breads among family members and invite everyone to share the bread.

LEADER: Now we will pass the basket of breads around. When you pass the basket, offer it, saying, "Jesus is the Bread of Life." When you receive the basket, respond, "Thank you."

ALL: *Take a piece or several pieces of bread, pass the basket to another person, and then eat the bread.*

Closing

LEADER: God, our loving Father,
all our blessings are from you.
Today we celebrate your love.
We gather to share the love you give us
    and to give you thanks.
Send us the Holy Spirit
to help us remember to give you thanks
    every day.
We ask this through Jesus Christ our Lord.

ALL: Amen.

We Remember

Think of a time that you spent with a loved one. What did it mean to be in that person's presence? Did time drag or seem to fly? Why was that? When we go to Mass to celebrate the Eucharist, we are spending time with God. Jesus is present with us. Joined to Jesus, we worship God through the power of the Holy Spirit.

At the Last Supper Jesus gave the Eucharist to the Church. The bread he gave us was his Body and the cup of wine was his Blood, poured out for the forgiveness of sin. We believe that under the appearances of bread and wine, Jesus is really and truly present with us. Through the celebration of this sacrificial meal we share in the life, Death, and Resurrection of Jesus. We join Jesus in his self-sacrificing love.

Overview

What We Will Learn

In your time together your family will deepen its understanding and living of the Church's faith. The faith theme of this lesson is:

Jesus instituted the Eucharist at the Last Supper.

What We Will Do

Follow these simple steps to help your child prepare for the celebration of the sacrament. The details of this process are found on page 30 of this family guide.

- **Preparation:** Read and reflect on the background essay on page 28. Look over he "Overview" page.

- **Step One:** Celebrate and share your experience of the ritual action of proclaiming an acclamation. The ritual is found on page 31 of this family guide.

- **Step Two:** Retell and share your understanding of the Scripture story "The Last Supper" (see Luke 22:17–20). An adapted version of the Scripture story is found on page 40 of your child's *Eucharist* book.

- **Step Three:** Discuss and share how your family can participate more fully in praying the Eucharistic Prayer. The Church's teaching on the Eucharistic Prayer is found on pages 42 and 43 in your child's *Eucharist* book.

- **Step Four:** Choose to make a difference in your own lives and in the lives of others by doing and saying things that give evidence of your belief in the presence of Jesus with you. Suggested activities are found on pages 44 and 45 of your child's *Eucharist* book.

- **Conclusion:** Pray together for guidance and help in living your faith. A suggested prayer is found on page 30 of this family guide.

What We Will Need

These are the items you will need for this lesson. Take the time to gather them in advance of meeting with your child:

- RCL Benziger's *Eucharist* child's book
- Unleavened bread and grapes
- Family Bible or a children's version of the Bible
- Scripture card "The Last Supper"
- Pencils

Looking for More

These are some additional resources that will help you enrich or extend the lesson:

- RCL Benziger's *Eucharist* music CD, Song 9, "Cristo Ha Muerto"; Song 10, "Cantamos Amen (We Sing Amen)"; Song 11, "We Remember You"; Song 12, "Love Each Other."

- **Children's Books**

  —*Nadia the Willful* by Sue Alexander (Pantheon Books). Keeping a loving memory alive through sharing and love.

  —*Wilfrid Gordon McDonald Partridge* by Mem Fox (Kane/Miller Book Publishers.) A story that reminds us of the meaning of memory.

- **Children's Videos**

  —**Faith First** Grade 2 video, Segment 7, The Visual Bible™, "The Lord's Supper."

  —*Last Supper* (Brown-ROA).

- RCL Benziger's *Eucharist* interactive calendar.

 Visit the RCL Benziger sacraments Web site at rclbsacraments.com.

Sharing Together

STEP ONE
Celebrate the Ritual

- Celebrate the ritual "Remembering Jesus."
- Invite everyone to share what it was like to experience the family ritual. Be sure to affirm all responses.
- Open the child's book to pages 38 and 39. Ask your child to describe what they see happening in the photographs.
- Read, discuss, and complete the rest of page 39.

STEP TWO
Share the Scripture Story

- Look at the illustration on pages 40 and 41. Ask your child to describe what they see happening in the illustration.
- Point out the "Faith Focus" question. Ask your child to listen for the answer as they listen to the Scripture story.
- Read, discuss, and complete pages 40 and 41. Pay special attention to "Together as a Family."

STEP THREE
Discover the Faith of the Church

- Look at the photographs on pages 42 and 43. Ask your child to describe what they see happening in the pictures.
- Read the "Faith Focus" question. Ask your child to listen for the answer as you read these pages.
- Read, discuss, and complete pages 42 and 43. Pay special attention to "Together as a Family."
- Help your child discover how the different names the Church gives to the Eucharist help them come to a better understanding of the Eucharist.
- You might like to use pages 67 and 68 of the child's book to help your child better understand and become familiar with the rites and prayers of the Eucharistic Prayer.

STEP FOUR
Make a Difference

- Read, discuss, and complete page 44. Encourage everyone to share a faith choice.
- Read, discuss, and complete page 45. Choose one activity from "Sharing Together" that will help you live your faith as a family.
- Turn to the back of the child's book and punch out the Scripture card "The Last Supper." Talk about the card and where you can keep it to serve as a reminder of this lesson and your time together.

Closing Prayer

Conclude your time together by using this prayer or one of your own choosing. Begin by signing yourselves, praying,

ALL: In the name of the Father, and of the Son, and of the Holy Spirit. Amen.

LEADER: Let us proclaim the mystery of faith.

ALL: When we eat this Bread and drink this Cup, we proclaim your Death, O Lord, until you come again.

LEADER: By his Death and Resurrection, Jesus has shown God's great love for us. May the love of God fill our hearts.

ALL: Amen.

LEADER: May the Holy Spirit help us share God's love with others.

ALL: Amen.

LEADER: May almighty God bless us, the Father, and the Son, and the Holy Spirit.

ALL: Amen.

LEADER: Go in peace, glorifying the Lord by your life.

ALL: Thanks be to God.

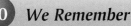

Remembering Jesus

Gathering

Gather your family around a table on which you have placed bread and grapes. Invite everyone to settle themselves and to become aware of God's presence. After a moment of quiet, begin the celebration of the ritual.

LEADER: Let us begin as we were baptized by praying the Sign of the Cross.

ALL: *Making the Sign of the Cross, pray,*
In the name of the Father,
and of the Son,
and of the Holy Spirit. Amen.

LEADER: God, our loving Father,
you are with us as we gather
to remember your Son, Jesus.
Send the Holy Spirit to open our hearts
to listen to your presence with us.
We ask this through Jesus Christ our Lord.

ALL: Amen.

Scripture Reading

Proclaim or invite someone to proclaim the Scripture story "The Last Supper" (see Luke 22:17–20) from your family Bible. An adapted version of the Scripture story is found on page 40 of your child's Eucharist book.

LEADER: God is with us in a special way
when we listen to his Word, the Bible.
Let us make a sign of the cross on our forehead, lips, and over our heart and ask the Holy Spirit to help us listen to the Word of God.

READER: A reading from the holy Gospel according to Luke.

ALL: *Reverently make the sign of the cross on their forehead, lips, and over their heart, saying,*
Glory to you, O Lord.

READER: *Proclaim the Scripture. Conclude the reading, saying,*
The Gospel of the Lord.

ALL: Praise to you, Lord Jesus Christ.

Ritual

Point out that when we gather as a community for Mass, we come together to remember Jesus' life, Death, and Resurrection. During the Eucharistic Prayer, we pray or sing the Memorial Acclamation.

LEADER: Repeat after me as we pray the Memorial Acclamation. *(You may say or sing this acclamation.)*

LEADER: When we eat this Bread

ALL: When we eat this Bread

LEADER: and drink this Cup,

ALL: and drink this Cup,

LEADER: we proclaim your Death, O Lord,

ALL: we proclaim your Death, O Lord,

LEADER: until you come again.

ALL: until you come again.

Closing

LEADER: God, our loving Father,
today we gather to remember your Son, Jesus Christ.
We know that Jesus is always with us.
Send us the Holy Spirit
to help us live as Jesus taught us.
We ask this through Jesus Christ our Lord.

ALL: Amen.

CHAPTER 6

We Celebrate

How present are we to our families? How present are we to our children? Being totally present to another person is a gift. Being totally present to others, as they need us, is to image God to others. As parents, we can evaluate our presence with our children. How responsive are we? How much do we truly value our time with our children? Are we so busy fulfilling our schedules that we end up just going through the motions of being present to them?

Jesus said, "I am the bread of life. . . . Those who eat my flesh and drink my blood live in me, and I in them" (based on John 6:35, 56). Jesus is present with us at Mass. The consecrated bread is the Body of Christ. The consecrated wine is the Blood of Christ. Through our sharing the one bread and the one cup, we are made one with Jesus and one with his Body, the Church (see 1 Corinthians 10:17).

Overview

What We Will Learn

In your time together your family will deepen its understanding and living of the Church's faith. The faith theme of this lesson is:

Sharing the Eucharist in Holy Communion strengthens our union with Christ and with the church community.

What We Will Do

Follow these simple steps to help your child prepare for the celebration of the sacrament. The details of this process are found on page 34 of this family guide.

- **Preparation:** Read and reflect on the background essay on page 32. Look over the "Overview" page.

- **Step One:** Celebrate and share your experience of the ritual action of sharing a sign of the peace of Christ. The ritual is found on page 35 of this family guide.

- **Step Two:** Retell and share your understanding of the Scripture story "The Road to Emmaus" (see Luke 24:13–35). An adapted version of the Scripture story is found on page 48 of your child's *Eucharist* book.

- **Step Three:** Discuss and share how your family can participate more fully in the Communion Rite. The Church's teaching on the Communion Rite is found on pages 50 and 51 of your child's *Eucharist* book.

- **Step Four:** Choose to make a difference in your own lives and in the lives of others by living as peacemakers. Suggested activities are found on pages 52 and 53 of your child's *Eucharist* book.

- **Conclusion:** Pray together asking God for his blessing. A suggested prayer is found on page 34 of this family guide.

What We Will Need

These are the items you will need for this lesson. Take the time to gather them in advance of meeting with your child:

- RCL Benziger's *Eucharist* child's book
- Family Bible or children's version of the Bible
- Candle
- Scripture card "The Road to Emmaus"
- Pencils

Looking for More

These are some additional resources to help you enrich or extend the lesson:

- RCL Benziger's *Eucharist* music CD, Song 13, "The Lord's Prayer"; Song 14, "Taste and See"; Song 15, "Pan de Vida."

- **Children's Books**
  —*Bread, Bread, Bread* by Ann Morris (Morrow, William & Co.). A celebration of the many different kinds of bread and how they can be enjoyed.
  —*The Unbeatable Bread* by Lyn Littlefield Hoopes (Dial Books for Young Readers). The aroma of special bread draws people to unite in a feast.

- **Children's Videos**
  —**Faith First** Grade 3 video, Segment 8, "The Our Father."
  —*First Eucharist* (Franciscan Media).

- RCL Benziger's *Eucharist* interactive calendar.

 Visit the RCL Benziger sacraments Web site at rclbsacraments.com.

Sharing Together

STEP ONE
Celebrate the Ritual

- Celebrate the ritual "Sharing the Presence of Christ."
- Invite everyone to share what it was like to experience the family ritual. Be sure to affirm all responses.
- Open the child's book to pages 46 and 47. Ask your child to describe what they see happening in the photographs.
- Read, discuss, and complete the rest of page 47.

STEP TWO
Share the Scripture Story

- Look at the illustration on pages 48 and 49. Ask your child to describe what they see happening in the illustration.
- Point out the "Faith Focus" question. Ask your child to listen for the answer as they listen to the Scripture story.
- Read, discuss, and complete pages 48 and 49. Pay special attention to "Together as a Family."

STEP THREE
Discover the Faith of the Church

- Look at the photographs on pages 50 and 51. Ask your child to describe what they see happening in the pictures.
- Read the "Faith Focus" question. Ask your child to listen for the answer as you read.
- Read, discuss, and complete pages 50 and 51. Pay special attention to "Together as a Family."
- Emphasize that the consecrated bread and consecrated wine we receive at Mass are really and truly the Body and Blood of Christ.
- You might like to use pages 69–71 of your child's *Eucharist* book to help your child better understand and become familiar with the rites and prayers of the Communion Rite of the Mass.

STEP FOUR
Make a Difference

- Read, discuss, and complete page 52. Encourage everyone to share a faith choice.
- Read, discuss, and complete page 53. Choose one activity from "Sharing Together" that will help you live your faith as a family.
- Turn to the back of the child's book and punch out the Scripture card "The Road to Emmaus." Talk about the card and where you can keep it to serve as a reminder of this lesson and your time together.

Closing Prayer

Conclude your time together by using this prayer or one of your own choosing. Begin by signing yourselves, praying,

ALL: In the name of the Father, and of the Son, and of the Holy Spirit. Amen.

LEADER: God, our loving Father, gives us food from Heaven, the Bread of Life. May the Lord bless us and keep us.

ALL: Amen.

LEADER: May his face shine upon us and be gracious to us.

ALL: Amen.

LEADER: May he look upon us with kindness and give us his peace.

ALL: Amen.

LEADER: May almighty God bless us, the Father, and the Son, and the Holy Spirit.

ALL: Amen.

LEADER: Go in peace, glorifying the Lord by your life.

ALL: Thanks be to God.

Sharing the Presence of Christ

Gathering

Gather your family around a table where you have placed a lit candle. Invite everyone to settle themselves and to become aware of God's presence. After a moment of quiet, begin the celebration of the ritual.

LEADER: Let us begin as we were baptized.

ALL: *Making the sign of the cross, pray,*
In the name of the Father,
and of the Son,
and of the Holy Spirit. Amen.

LEADER: God, our loving Father,
you give us the gift of new life in Jesus,
  your Son.
Send us the Holy Spirit
to open our hearts to your Word
and to help us share the gift of Jesus
  with others.
We ask this through Jesus Christ our Lord.

ALL: Amen.

Scripture Reading

Proclaim or invite someone to proclaim the Scripture story "The Road to Emmaus" (see Luke 24:13–35) from your family Bible. An adapted version of the Scripture story is found on page 48 of your child's Eucharist *book.*

LEADER: Let us ask the Holy Spirit to help us listen to the Word of God.

READER: A reading from the holy Gospel according to Luke.

ALL: *Reverently make the sign of the cross on their forehead, lips, and over their heart, saying,*
Glory to you, O Lord.

READER: *Proclaim the Scripture. Conclude the reading, saying,*
The Gospel of the Lord.

ALL: Praise to you, Lord Jesus Christ.

Ritual

Point out that at church, the Easter candle reminds us of the life, Death, and Resurrection of Jesus. The light of the Easter candle reminds us that Jesus is present with us.

LEADER: To celebrate that Jesus is with us, let us pray the prayer Jesus gave us.

ALL: Our Father . . .

LEADER: Jesus gave us the gift of peace. Let us share Christ's peace with one another.

ALL: *Share a sign of peace.*

Closing

LEADER: God, our loving Father,
you have given us the gift of your Son,
  Jesus Christ.
Send us the Holy Spirit
to help us share Christ's love and peace
  with others.
We ask this through Jesus Christ our Lord.

ALL: Amen.

We Live

At Baptism we were joined to Christ, were made sharers in the divine life, and received the gift of the Holy Spirit. The Holy Spirit is our companion and guide. The Holy Spirit strengthens us and encourages us to live as followers of Christ. The Holy Spirit helps us continue Christ's work in the world. Through Baptism we are called to love and serve God and one another. Receiving Eucharist strengthens us to live our call to such a life.

Children are often inadvertently taught that the work of the Church is for adults. As your child continues the sacramental process of initiation into the Church, be sure to help your child discover their own unique gifts that can be shared with others. Children who grow up participating in a life of service are more likely to live lives of service as adults.

Overview

What We Will Learn

In your time together your family will deepen its understanding and living of the Church's faith. The faith theme of this lesson is:

> Sharing the Eucharist strengthens us to live as disciples of Christ and share in the mission of the Church.

What We Will Do

Follow these simple steps to help your child prepare for the celebration of the sacrament. The details of this process are found on page 38 of this family guide.

- **Preparation:** Read and reflect on the background essay on page 36. Look over the "Overview" page.

- **Step One:** Celebrate and share your experience of the ritual action of anointing with oil. The ritual is found on page 39 of this family guide.

- **Step Two:** Retell and share your understanding of the Scripture story "The Gift of the Holy Spirit" (see Acts of the Apostles 1:12, 2:1–42). An adapted version of the Scripture story is found on page 56 of your child's *Eucharist* book.

- **Step Three:** Discuss and share how your family can participate more fully in the Concluding Rites of the Mass. The Church's teaching on the Concluding Rites of the Mass is found on pages 58 and 59 in your child's book.

- **Step Four:** Choose to make a difference in your own lives and in the lives of others. Do one thing that tells other people about Jesus. Suggested activities are found on pages 60 and 61 in your child's book.

- **Conclusion:** Pray together for guidance and help in living your faith. A suggested prayer is found on page 38 of this family guide.

What We Will Need

These are the items you will need for this lesson. Take the time to gather them in advance of meeting with your child:

- RCL Benziger's *Eucharist* child's book

- A small, clear glass bowl; olive oil; fragrance to mix with the oil

- Family Bible or a children's version of the Bible

- Scripture card "The Gift of the Holy Spirit"

- Pencils

Looking for More

These are some suggestions to help you enrich or extend the lesson:

- RCL Benziger's *Eucharist* music CD, Song 16, "We Are the Church"; Song 17, "Together We'll Share."

- **Children's Books**
  - *City Green* by DyAnne DiSalvio-Ryan (Morrow Junior Books). A girl starts a campaign to clean up an empty lot and turn it into a community garden.
  - *Uncle Willy and the Soup Kitchen* by DyAnne DiSalvio-Ryan (Morrow Junior Books). A boy discovers why somebody would want to work in a soup kitchen.

- **Children's Videos**
  - **Faith First** Grade 2 video, Segment 1, "Bible Songs"; Segment 3, "The Story of a Saint."
  - **Faith First** Grade 4 video, Segment 3, "Story of Faith."

- RCL Benziger's *Eucharist* interactive calendar.

 Visit the RCL Benziger sacraments Web site at rclbsacraments.com.

Sharing Together

STEP ONE
Celebrate the Ritual

- Celebrate the ritual "Anointing with Oil."
- Invite everyone to share what it was like to experience the family ritual. Be sure to affirm all responses.
- Open the child's book to pages 54 and 55. Ask your child to describe what they see happening in the photographs.
- Read, discuss, and complete the rest of page 55.

STEP TWO
Share the Scripture Story

- Look at the illustration on pages 56 and 57. Ask your child to describe what is happening in the illustration.
- Point out the "Faith Focus" question. Ask your child to listen for the answer as the Scripture story is read.
- Read, discuss, and complete pages 56 and 57. Pay special attention to "Together as a Family."

STEP THREE
Discover the Faith of the Church

- Look at the photographs on pages 58 and 59. Ask your child to describe what they see happening in the pictures.
- Read the "Faith Focus" question. Ask your child to listen for the answer as you read.
- Read, discuss, and complete pages 58 and 59. Explain that the word *Mass* comes from a word that means "to be sent out." Pay special attention to "Together as a Family."
- You might like to use page 71 of your child's *Eucharist* book to help your child better understand and become familiar with the rites and prayers of the Concluding Rites of the Mass.

STEP FOUR
Make a Difference

- Read, discuss, and complete page 60. Encourage everyone to share a faith choice.
- Read, discuss, and complete page 61. Choose one activity from "Sharing Together" that will help you live your faith as a family.
- Turn to the back of the child's book and punch out the Scripture card "The Gift of the Holy Spirit." Talk about the card and where you can keep it to serve as a reminder of this lesson and your time together.

Closing Prayer

Conclude your time together by using this prayer or one of your own choosing. Begin by signing yourselves, praying,

ALL: In the name of the Father, and of the Son, and of the Holy Spirit. Amen.

LEADER: May the Holy Spirit be with us to help us live our lives every day.

ALL: Amen.

LEADER: May almighty God bless us, the Father, and the Son, and the Holy Spirit.

ALL: Amen.

LEADER: Go in peace, glorifying the Lord by your life.

ALL: Thanks be to God.

Anointing with Oil

Gathering

Gather your family at a table on which you have placed a small glass bowl of fragrant oil. Invite everyone to settle themselves and to become aware of God's presence. After a moment of quiet, begin the celebration of the ritual.

LEADER: Let us begin as we were baptized.

ALL: *Making the Sign of the Cross, pray,*
In the name of the Father,
and of the Son,
and of the Holy Spirit. Amen.

LEADER: God, our loving Father,
you give us the Holy Spirit
   as our Helper and Guide.
Send us the Holy Spirit
to open our hearts to listen
   to your Word.
We ask this in the name of Jesus Christ,
   your Son.

ALL: Amen.

Scripture Reading

Proclaim or invite someone to proclaim the Scripture story "The Gift of the Holy Spirit" (see Acts of the Apostles 1:12, 2:1–42) from your family Bible. An adapted version of the Scripture story is found on page 56 of your child's Eucharist book.

LEADER: Let us make the sign of the cross on our forehead, lips, and over our heart and ask the Holy Spirit to help us listen to the Word of God.

READER: A reading from the Acts of the Apostles.
Proclaim the Scripture. Conclude the reading, saying,
The word of the Lord.

ALL: Thanks be to God.

Ritual

Explain that you will anoint the palms of each person's hands with oil, making the sign of the cross while you say, "You have the gift of the Holy Spirit. Go in peace, glorifying the Lord by your life." Point out that all will respond, "Thanks be to God," as they rub their hands together, rubbing the oil into their hands.

LEADER: *In a small glass bowl, which you have placed on the table, mix olive oil and a few drops of a fragrant oil. Dip the thumb of your right hand into the oil. Then make the sign of the cross on the palms of each person's hands, saying,*
(Name), you have the gift of the Holy Spirit. Go in peace, glorifying the Lord by your life.

ALL: *Rubbing their hands together, respond,*
Thanks be to God.

Closing

LEADER: God, our loving Father,
today our hands were anointed with oil.
We were reminded that at Baptism
we received the gift of the the Holy Spirit
and were anointed as followers of your Son.
Thank you for the gift of the Holy Spirit
who helps us live as Jesus taught us.
We make our prayer in the name of Jesus
   Christ our Lord.

ALL: Amen.

rclbsacraments.com
Click on *"Eucharist"*

RCL Benziger's "Sacraments" Web site enriches and expands RCL Benziger's *Eucharist* and *Reconciliation* programs.

The Web Site:

- provides parents and children the opportunity to have fun and engage in activities that connect to their immediate sacrament preparation;

- gives parents the opportunity to explore further their role with their children in sacrament preparation;

- supports catechists with additional resources.

Visit RCL Benziger's "Sacraments" Web site at **rclbsacraments.com**. It will reveal the menu of activities and options for children, young people, parents, and catechists. Here are some things you will find on the Web site that will enrich and expand preparation for Eucharist:

For Parents and Families

- Chapter-related Activites for Children

- Activities for Parents and Children

- Scripture Stories

- Mealtime Prayers

- Reflection Questions

- Frequently Asked Questions

For Catechists and Program Directors

- Chapter-related Activites for Children

- Materials for Preparing Older Children

- Catechist Orientation and Ongoing Formation

- Program Director Resources